You asked for it SERIES

WIFE

barbara rainey

How can I become a *dynamite* wife?

FAMILYLIFE
Bringing Timeless Principles Home

WIFE: How can I become a *dynamite* wife?

Copyright © 2003 FamilyLife. All rights reserved.
No part of this publication may be reproduced, stored in a retrieval system, or transmitted in any form or by any means—electronic, mechanical, photocopy, recording, or otherwise—without the prior written permission of the publisher.

Published by FamilyLife, a division of Campus Crusade for Christ.

Author: Barbara Rainey
Senior Editor: David Boehi
Project Coordinator: Betty Rogers
Editing: Susan Matthews, Dale Walters
Graphic Designer: Jennifer I. Smith
Cover Photography: Jennifer I. Smith

Printed in the United States of America.
ISBN 1572294795
UPC 61592707646

Unless otherwise noted, Scripture quotations are taken from the New American Standard Bible.
Copyright © 1960, 1962, 1963, 1968, 1971, 1972, 1973, 1975, 1977, 1994 by The Lockman Foundation. All rights reserved. Used by permission.

FAMILYLIFE™
Bringing Timeless Principles Home

Dennis Rainey, President
5800 Ranch Drive Little Rock, Arkansas 72223
1-800-FL-TODAY (358-6329) 24 Hours a Day
www.familylife.com
A division of Campus Crusade for Christ

RELEVANT ISSUES, PRACTICAL ANSWERS

For years you've been asking us questions about the issues that concern you and your family. Some of these questions reflect the normal concerns and problems that most families face every day.

WIFE: How can I become a dynamite wife?

And some echo the anxiety of husbands and wives, fathers and mothers who see their most important relationships beginning to unravel.

Because you asked for it, we're responding ... with a series of mini-books answering the most-asked questions that come to us by providing biblical blueprints for building godly homes. We hope our replies give you hope by pointing you to the God who created us.

Dennis and Barbara Rainey

SPECIAL NOTE: For further biblical understanding about the complementary roles and responsibilities of husbands and wives, we suggest you also read Dennis' answer to the question, "What should be the husband's 'role' in marriage? A wife's responsibilities can be properly understood only in the context of loving, servant leadership by her husband.

WHAT SHOULD BE THE WIFE'S "ROLE" IN MARRIAGE?

by Barbara Rainey

Perhaps more than at any other time in history, women today need a clear understanding of how they should relate to their husbands. In fact, the significant social changes brought about by the women's movement over the last few decades have led to such confusion that the very idea of "roles" is repugnant to some. They feel as if somehow they lose their identity and their freedom if they adhere to some type of outdated standard.

It's important for us to look clearly at what the Bible says on this subject. And while the Bible doesn't apply our modern word "role" to marriage, the Scriptures are clear about the unique responsibilities God assigns to a wife.

BIBLICAL RESPONSIBILITIES FOR WIVES

Responsibility #1 Be Helpers to Our Husbands

While all of us are called to be helpers to others, the Bible places a special emphasis on this responsibility for wives. Genesis tells us that God realized it wasn't good for man to be alone, and that He decided to make a "helper suitable for him" (Genesis 2:18). It is interesting to note that the Hebrew meaning of the word helper in this passage is found hereafter in the Bible to refer only to God as He helps us. The fact that this same word is applied to a wife signifies that we women have been given tremendous power for good in our husbands' lives. God has designed wives to help their husbands become all that God intends for them to be.

Responsibilty #2: Respect Our Husbands

In Ephesians 5:33, Paul says, "...the wife must respect her husband." When you respect your husband, you give him reverence, notice him, regard him, honor him, prefer him, and esteem him. It means valuing his opinion, admiring his wisdom and character, appreciating his commitment to you, and considering his needs and values.

One way to respect your husband is to consider and understand the weight of his responsibilities. It is easy to look at your husband and see what is wrong instead of what he does right. As someone once said, "Faults are like the headlights of your car—those of others seem more glaring."

WIFE: How can I become a dynamite wife?

Our husbands have many needs. The "macho man" who is self-contained, independent, and invulnerable is a myth. One day Dennis gave me a list of what he considered to be some of the primary needs most men have:

- Self-confidence in his personhood as a man
- To be listened to
- Companionship
- To be needed

To me, meeting these needs is what respecting your husband is all about. To bolster Dennis' confidence, for example, I try to encourage him by being his number one fan. Every husband wants his wife to be on his team, to coach him when necessary, but most of all to be his cheerleader. A husband needs a wife who is behind him, believing in him, appreciating him, and cheering him on as he goes out into the world every day.

Some of you may be thinking, "I can't think of anything to respect in my husband." Perhaps you are like the young mother I know whose husband drank heavily and spent little time with the children. She had a difficult time viewing him with respect and honor. A deliberate change of focus from his weaknesses to his few strengths enabled her to begin to see her spouse in a positive light. Gaining a better perspective may aid you in esteeming your husband, too.

When photographing an extensive landscape, it's impossible to focus simultaneously on the flowers in the foreground and the mountains in the background. So the photographer adjusts the camera lens to bring his chosen subject into focus. If he focuses on the flowers, for example, the mountains become fuzzy.

Similarly, in viewing your husband, you must choose your focus. Continually concentrating on his flaws will negatively affect your overall perception of him. Yet it is possible to blur the image of some weaknesses so that you notice them less and learn to focus sharply on the positive qualities, causing genuine respect to develop. Philippians 4:8 tells us: "Whatever is true, whatever is honorable, whatever is right, whatever is pure, whatever is lovely, whatever is of good repute, if there is any excellence and if anything is worthy of praise, let your mind dwell on these things."

Responsibilty #3: Love Our Husbands

Titus 2:4 calls for wives to love their husbands. A good description of the kind of love your husband needs is "unconditional acceptance." In other words, accept your husband just as he is—an imperfect person.

Love also means being committed to a mutually fulfilling sexual relationship. I realize there is a whole lot more to love than sex, but we are looking at how to fulfill God's command to love our husbands. Therefore, we must look at love from their perspective, not just our own.

Surveys show that sex is one of a man's most important needs—if not *the* most important.

When a wife resists intimacy, is disinterested, or is only passively interested, her husband may feel rejection. It will cut at his self-image, tear at him to the very center of his being, and create isolation.

A friend shared something with me that I believe is profound. In order to put the sexual dimension of a man in perspective, she said, it's important to realize he can meet many of his needs apart from you. He can send his clothes to a laundry, eat all of his meals out, get companionship with friends, receive acceptance and respect at work, and find a listening ear from a counselor, and in all those activities he can stay in the center of God's will. But if he meets his sexual needs with someone other than his wife, it is sin.

My husband's sexual needs should be more important and higher on my priority list than menus, housework, projects, activities, and even the children. It does not mean that I should think about sex all day and every day, but it does mean that I find ways to remember my husband and his needs. It means I save some of my energy for him. It keeps me from being selfish and living only for my own needs and wants. Maintaining that focus helps me defeat isolation in our marriage.

I believe one reason there are so many affairs, even among Christians, is that too many Christian wives do not value their husband's genuine *physical* need. By rejecting them at that point, wives severely undermine their confidence and trust in your love. You must accept and respect this important part of your husband's masculinity. If you do not love and accept him in this area, your other demonstrations of love will be hollow.

Another way to love your husband is accepting the lifestyle that comes with his schedule.

For many years earlier in our marriage, I had to learn to be content with a schedule that did not allow me to spend summers gardening. For years, every spring I bought seeds and planted beds of flowers and a few vegetables. Then, about June 1, we packed up and left for most of the summer for Dennis' teaching assignments, conferences, and meetings, and my garden never lasted. We also had to learn how to live out of a suitcase and even out of the car a great deal of the time.

Although I have not always enjoyed the

consequences of our schedule—the stress of traveling with our brood, packing and unpacking repeatedly, finding someone to watch and care for our home, etc.—I never criticized Dennis about it. My husband's schedule is important to me. I choose to go with him to be a part of what he does, to watch and help and be available for him. I know he needs me and I want to be there.

Responsibilty #4: Submit to the Leadership of Our Husbands

I'm going to discuss this responsibility at greater length than the others—not because it is more important but because it is more controversial. Just mention the word "submission," and many women immediately become angry and even hostile. This controversial concept has been highly debated and misunderstood.

Some husbands and wives actually believe submission indicates that women are inferior to men in some way. I have known women who think that if they submit they will lose their identity and become "non-persons." Others fear (some with good reason) that submission leads to being used or abused.

Another misconception is that submission means blind obedience on the part of the woman. She can give no input to her husband, question nothing, and only stay obediently barefoot and pregnant in the kitchen.

A few years ago during a FamilyLife Weekend to Remember™, I received a letter from a wife in attendance that illustrates how confusing submission can be to some women. She had been married a little over 10 years and told me: "As you pray for miracles after this conference, please pray for one in my corner." In her letter she wrote, "I always thought that God's idea of submission was pretty much to do whatever, whenever, and however I was told—basically, a master/slave relationship. In the last year, I have been discovering that this is not what God had in mind."

What does God have in mind? Here are two passages from Scripture:

> *Wives, be subject to your husbands, as is fitting in the Lord. Husbands, love your wives and do not be embittered against them.*
>
> — Colossians 3:18-19

> *Wives, be subject to your own husbands, as to the Lord. For the husband is the head of the wife, as Christ also is the head of the church, He Himself being the Savior of the body. But as the church is subject to Christ, so also the wives ought to be to their husbands in everything. Husbands, love your wives, just as Christ also loved the church and gave Himself up for her, so that He might sanctify*

her, having cleansed her by the washing of water with the word, that He might present to Himself the church in all her glory, having no spot or wrinkle or any such thing; but that she would be holy and blameless. So, husbands ought also to love their own wives as their own bodies. He who loves his own wife loves himself; for no one ever hated his own flesh, but nourishes and cherishes it, just as Christ also does the church, because we are members of His body.

— Ephesians 5:22-30

These Scriptures make it clear that a wife should submit voluntarily to her husband's sensitive and loving leadership. The Greek word used in the New Testament for submission is *hupotasso*, which means "to voluntarily complete, arrange, adapt or blend so as to make a complete whole or complete pattern." As I voluntarily submit to my husband, I am completing him. I am helping him fulfill his responsibilities, and I am helping him become the man, the husband, and the leader God intended him to be.

Building oneness in marriage works best when both partners choose to fulfill their responsibilities voluntarily, with no pressure or coercion. To become the servant-leader God has commanded him to be, Dennis needs my gracious respect and submission. And when Dennis loves me the way he is commanded to, I can more easily submit myself to that leadership.

I do this with an attitude of entrusting myself to God. In one of his letters, Peter told us that even though Jesus suffered terrible pain and insults,

He did not retaliate "but kept entrusting Himself to Him who judges righteously" (1 Peter 2:23). When you entrust your life to the Father, it's much easier to be the wife of an imperfect man, particularly when you may have disagreements.

The following chart compares the world's concept of submission with the concept in Scripture.

Two Views of Submission

WORLD'S VIEW OF SUBMISSION	SCRIPTURAL VIEW
Non-resistant	Loyal
Unassertive	Completing
Bowing	Humble
Cowering	Obliging
Subservient	Faithful
Second-class	Willing
No initiative	Flexible
No backbone	Consent to, agree to, defer to

How does this concept of responsibilities apply to decision-making in marriage? The first thing to know is that, when Dennis and I have a decision to make, we almost always make it by unanimous agreement. If we begin talking about a decision from opposite perspectives, we typically share our thoughts, come to an agreement, and the decision is made with oneness. It is rare for us to continue to disagree, but when we do, I feel Dennis should make the final decision.

When our oldest daughter, Ashley, was approaching her fifth birthday, we found ourselves facing our first schooling decision. Ashley's birthday is in late August, and in Arkansas that meant she would be the youngest child in her class.

I had enrolled her in an excellent pre-school program to help prepare her for kindergarten. The director of the nursery school, plus Ashley's teacher, said she had done beautifully in pre-school and would do just as well in kindergarten the next year. I agreed.

I came home and reported all these facts to Dennis. I laid it all out carefully and convincingly, I thought, but to my surprise, he did not agree. I could not believe that he was not buying my persuasive logic. He simply said, "I think we should hold her out for a year."

I pursued with my arguments: "She makes friends easily. The teachers all think she should be in school next year. Why can't you agree with me?"

Dennis could not really give me a reason. He just felt that Ashley should not go to school—even kindergarten—as a 5-year-old.

I backed off, waited a couple of weeks, prayed about it, and tried again. I presented all my facts, trying to beef up every point to make my position more convincing, but Dennis did not budge.

We went on like this for several weeks, and I realized I was not making any progress. I was becoming more entrenched in my position, and he was likewise immovable in his. In a word, we had reached an impasse.

I decided I had to do something, so I prayed and said, "Okay, Lord, I think I'm right, and he is wrong. I pray that You will change his mind—but Lord, if I am wrong and he is right—I want You to change *my* attitude. I am willing to do whatever You want me to do, but You know I think he is wrong."

To my surprise, what changed was *my* attitude and perspective. In the days that followed, God gave me peace. As my position softened, I began to see Ashley more objectively, as a little girl who needed another year to be a child without the pressures of school. It turned out that holding Ashley back a year and starting her in kindergarten as a young 6-year-old was one of the smartest things we ever did for her. We discovered several years later that Ashley is dyslexic, an inherited difficulty with reading, and the extra year at home gave her a much better chance to deal with learning to read.

I am glad the Lord broke our impasse by reminding me that I needed to have the right attitude. I needed to prayerfully trust God to bring my heart and Dennis' in line with His will.

Decision making for the Christian couple should not be reduced to an issue of who is right and who is wrong. In those rare situations when we disagree, I am glad that Dennis and I have a biblically based structure that enables us to decide and move forward. It has meant that he must assume his responsibility as head of the home, but in assuming that position, he has learned that the role of a leader is that of a servant. As he serves me by listening to my perspective and really taking into consideration my advice, he has made my submission to him easier. I didn't say it was easy—just easier.

HOW IT ALL FITS TOGETHER

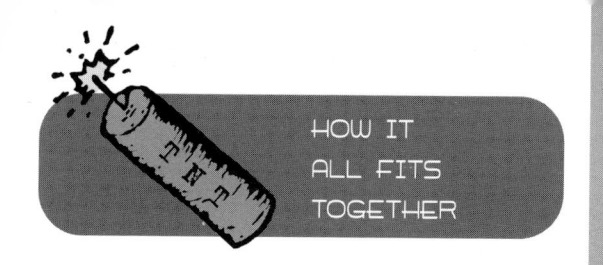

If you have ever sewn a dress, or attempted to sew one, you know how a pattern works. The pattern is made of many pieces, some large and some small, none of which accurately resembles the finished product.

When you lay out the pattern and cut the cloth, you do not have a garment but only some scraps of cloth. When it is properly assembled and made usable with buttons, a zipper, or snaps, these pieces make a complete dress.

Every pattern has pairs of parts: two sleeves, two bodice pieces, a front and back skirt, and even the collar and facing pieces are usually in two's. A marriage is very similar. God has designed a master pattern for husbands and wives, that when followed, will create a whole, usable, beautiful marriage.

In the same way a dress can be made in a variety of sizes and colors with numerous differences in detail from one pattern, so my marriage may look different from yours. As we acknowledge Christ as Lord of our lives, we must work out our marriages according to God's plan. The key is for each wife to follow God's plan, know her part, and work to fit in with her husband's responsibilities.

I have experienced many frustrations trying to fulfill my part of the marriage pattern with my husband's.

I have felt at times that it was too hard. I heard a verse in a sermon, seemingly unrelated to marriage, that clearly addresses this concern: God says, "What I am commanding you today is not too difficult for you or beyond your reach" (Deuteronomy 30:11).

I know by faith and by experience that God's plan for me as a wife does not restrict my creativity in expressing who I am. If I trust Him, the finished product is a life that reflects the full beauty that its Creator intended. When this becomes a reality for me as a wife, I experience oneness with God, oneness with my husband, and real freedom to be all that God created me to be.

A Special Note: Some of you may live with abuse or in excessively unhealthy and destructive conditions in your marriage. At times, it may be inappropriate or even life-threatening for you to apply unquestioningly the principles of submission. For example, if you are being physically or verbally abused, you may need to take steps to protect yourself and your children. You may need to say to your husband, "I love you, but enough is enough." If you are in that situation, please discerningly seek out your pastor or someone wise who has been trained to help with your specific issue. Loving, forgiving, and submitting do not mean that you become a doormat or indefinitely tolerate significantly destructive behavior.

Please refer to page 32 to order "A Way of Hope". This resource offers hope and gives suggestions for how to move toward safety in your situation.

YOU asked for it SERIES

For years people have been asking FamilyLife questions about the issues that concern their families. We have responded with this series written by Dennis and Barbara Rainey.

Other titles in this *You Asked For It* series:

CONFLICT: Why do we fight? How do we *stop*?
ROMANCE: How can we add more *sizzle* in our marriage?
DIVORCE: Does God allow it in *my* case?
HUSBAND: How can I become a *leading man* in my marriage?
AFRAID TO LEAD?: How can I *encourage* my husband to desire more with God?
BIRDS 'N' BEES: How do I teach my children *God's design for sex*?
PEER PRESSURE: How do I *motivate* my children to build the best friendships?
TOGETHERNESS: How can we *heal* the isolation in our marriage?
TRIALS: How can my family *keep the faith* during suffering?

Future topics in this series:

REMARRIAGE: How can we make it work?
SINGLE PARENTING: How can I raise my children to be *whole and responsible*?
STEPPARENTING: How can I gain my stepchildren's *respect*?
ANGER: How can I stop before I explode?
SPANKING: Is it *harmful* to my child?
AFFAIRS: What do I do when my spouse has *cheated*?
PORNOGRAPHY: What can I do when I am *addicted* to it?

Do you need excellent resources?

Scripturally based, this book addresses the multi-faceted roles of a wife as well as her spiritual needs. This is an invaluable reference tool for Christian wives, single women, pastors, missionaries, and biblical counselors.

Each year, millions of women are abused in the one place they thought they would be safe…in their home. This resource offers hope that they can change their lives and it gives suggestions for how to move toward safety.

Item #5215

Item #5150

FAMILYLIFE
Bringing Timeless Principles Home

To order call 1-800-FL-TODAY, or visit www.familylife.com.